Heart Turned Back

BERTHA ROGERS

Bertha Rogers

*For dear Dorothy,
wonderful writer!
June 9, 2010
Happy Birthday*

salmonpoetry

Published in 2010 by
Salmon Poetry
Cliffs of Moher, County Clare, Ireland
Website: www.salmonpoetry.com
Email: info@salmonpoetry.com

ISBN 978-1-907056-26-0

Cover artwork: *"Roots" by Bertha Rogers*
Cover design & typesetting: *Siobhán Hutson*
Printed in England by imprint*digital*.net

For my wonderful husband, Ernest

And to the memory of Luke and Lily and Clymentine, dear dog-friends

Acknowledgements

Several of these poems first appeared or will appear (sometimes in a different form) in the following magazines, periodicals or anthologies:

Able Muse E-Zine (ablemuse.com), *Big City Lit E-Zine* (nycbigcitylit.com), *Blueline, Blueline Anthology* (Syracuse University Press, NY), *Buckle &, Calapooya Collage, Chance of a Ghost Anthology* (Helicon Nine Editions, MO), *Climate Controlled Anthology* (The Diagram Online), *Cimarron Review, Comstock Review, Confluence, Connecticut Review, Creeping Bent, Green Mountains Review, Higginsville Reader Review, Home Planet News, Karamu, Laurel Review, Louisville Review, Many Mountains Moving, Midwest Quarterly, Negative Capability, Nimrod International Journal of Prose and Poetry, Off the Coast, Phoebe, Pivot, PoetryBay E-Zine* (poetrybay.com), *Rain of Two Waters Anthology* (Headwaters Press, NYC), *Rattapallax, Roanoke Review, The Louisville Review, The MacGuffin, The Roanoke Review, The Word Thursdays Anthology, The Second Word Thursdays Anthology* (Bright Hill Press, NY), *Volume Number*, and *Yankee Magazine*.

"Crowd" and "Buck" first appeared in *A House of Corners* chapbook, winner of the *Maryland Poetry Review* and State Literary Society Poetry Competition (Three Conditions Press, Baltimore, 2000). "Rhomboid" won PhiloPhonema's 2002 Lyric Recovery Contest, selected by Alfred Corn. "Truck Stand" was selected by John Ashbery for inclusion in the Millay Colony's 30th Anniversary Celebration Exhibit, Albany International Airport, 2004. "County Meath, Ireland," and "The Corn Field" appeared in *Sleeper, You Wake* (Mellen Press, 1991). "The Fourth Beast" appeared in *The Fourth Beast* chapbook (Snark Publishing, IL, 2004).

The author is grateful for residencies at Hawthornden International Writers' Retreat, Scotland; Caldera, the MacDowell Colony, the Millay Colony for the Arts, Jentel, the David and Julia White Colony, and Hedgebrook; those amazing places provided time and space for writing and revising these poems.

Contents

ONE—*The Green Sea*

TWO—*Like Night*

THREE—*Landscape With Wings*

ONE
The Green Sea

The tumult in the heart
keeps asking questions.
And then it stops and undertakes to answer
in the same tone of voice.
No one could tell the difference.

—ELIZABETH BISHOP
from "Conversation"

The First Time

The first time I saw time bend was just beyond
the turn of 13. That sheer fabric broke
in the middle of normal's morning, while June sun
prospected the windows. I slipped through
its transparency, found another space
not far away, along the rampant creek.
The place I escaped—chaos, noise, debris.
I was forced to choose—that was clear—
and so found a home near rush and stone.
Yes, there was a copse. There was water,
slipping over, ensorcelled by those
very stones. Or the stones were, by water.
   I rested in that room, passed out of it only when
   I heard my father's voice. Came back home.

Landscape in October

Let us go forth into what waits—white sky,
red moon. Let us embrace each rickety
breeze as if it were a new lover, all
pheromones askew for this right moment.

Each heretofore unknown river wants us;
each tree wishes our flight past every
rent petal, cold-emboldened insect.
All piebald horses stand ready to cheer.

Why, then, do *we* hesitate? Even the
coyote running the ridge knows the repose
of butchery without reward.

This hooped October morning, ground clouds
squalling, leaves plummeting, offers its own
complex answer. *Give over*, it says; *give*.

When You Were Dead

The other day, I dreamt you were dead, and
I woke to laughing—my own voice, laughing,
in February's bed. Morning's light—
low, white, like slowed snow—overspread
the room. My breath was icy above quilts.
My good husband—his breath cold too, little
clouds of north wind—slept next to me, warm
in our own winter, our chosen, bed.

You may indeed be dead—or you may well
be laughing, rallying in another
woman's bed. I don't know, don't care—
but I must admit I'm still provoked
by the memory of your wintry wit,
glacial smile. I believe you know.

Mountain Sequence:
A Pantoum in Four Parts

I. December

The night wind is a slow, cold song; mean,
like a failed man. He pleads for gloves
each morning, but you can't forgive.
He slips out, among trees refusing the sun,

like a failed man. He pleads for gloves,
nostalgic flurries, warmth provided by you.
He slips out, among trees refusing the sun.
You find a new house, an old crone skirting

nostalgic flurries, warmth provided by you.
The frozen ground is stern. Wrapped in solitude,
you find a new house, an old crone skirting
your ride back to darkness. Every morning,

the frozen ground is stern. Wrapped in solitude,
the window dangles a hussy moon.
Your ride back to darkness every morning
feeds the frozen ridge. You wake hungry.

The window dangles a hussy moon.
Light enters through mountain briars,
feeding the frozen ridge. You wake hungry,
like bone-open trees, hands uncovered.

Light enters through mountain briars.
The night wind is a slow, cold song; mean,
like bone-open trees, hands uncovered
each morning. But you can't forgive.

II. January

Two jays perch, furtive and mute,
in the hawthorn. You try to credit the day
but only recognize January's high sky,
the shadows of stones curling at your feet.

In the hawthorn you try to credit the day,
your lost faith. The drifting fields own you.
How the shadows of stones curl at your feet!
Clouds process, strung like rosaries,

your lost faith. The drifting fields own you,
the wind prying shingles from your cloister.
Clouds process, strung like rosaries.
You burrow in your flannel but your dreams,

the wind prying shingles from your cloister,
overcome, coming from the sea sky.
You burrow in your flannel but your dreams
turn the world over, and you flail,

overcome. Coming from the sea sky,
the clouds, heavy with water, with claws,
turn the world over, and you flail.
Your veins still crave autumn,

the clouds, heavy with water, with claws.
Two jays perch, furtive and mute,
Your veins still crave autumn
but only recognize January's high sky.

III. February

Leaves bleed into stone, the dying rabbit's
prints measuring her last winter, torn heart.
She stomps once, twice on the crust, blends
her scream with the blizzard's, her ragged

prints measuring her last winter, torn heart,
the murder she must suffer,
her scream, the blizzard's; her ragged
weeping in the cold. You despise

the murder she must suffer.
Under the glare, the man pleads constancy,
weeping in the cold. You despise
his fingers; they unbutton another blouse.

Under the glare, the man pleads constancy.
The meadow surrenders; the sky sinks
his fingers. They unbutton another blouse,
memory of summer's leaning horizon.

The meadow surrenders; the sky sinks,
leaves bleed into stone—the dying rabbit's
memory of summer's leaning horizon.
She stomps once, twice, on the crust; blends.

IV. March

The deer lives in the center of the road.
The proximity of sky might be too much,
the violence of spring—green, stabbing dusk;
maples giving up blood; the lilac's knowledge.

The proximity of sky might be too much.
It may be, this is how comprehension begins—
maples giving up blood, the lilac's knowledge,
dawn's complexity, ruddy shoulders bending.

It may be, this is how comprehension begins.
The redwings returning all at once this year—
dawn's complexity, ruddy shoulders bending.
Oh, yes, I need my morning loneliness,

the redwings returning all at once this year.
I am addicted to sunrise; it is night that breaks.
Oh yes, I need my morning loneliness,
your body, absent from this too-wide bed.

I am addicted to sunrise. It is night that breaks
your unbearable, whispered words,
your body, absent from this too-wide bed.
When the moon rises, the valley forgets

your unbearable, whispered words;
the deer lives in the center of the road.
When the moon rises, the valley forgets
the violence of spring—green stabbing; dusk.

Verge

Here, I came running to the chain-linked fence;
gazed through its taut diamonds like a fly

measuring honey's lie—through each link
a faded face, sum diminished by drizzle.

I waited, right here, and watched November's trees
rampage this strange stockade, its corroded brink;

watched them find the light they needed—
I saw it!—green, glaucous, anonymous.

My time on earth ended here, where the grass forgot
its season and morning froze into evening.

I turned my face to facets, forcing my lips to fit.
Then I swallowed ice—tasted every *within*; all *ever after*.

What I Saw

A photograph of a bear hibernating
in fallen leaves. Her cubs,

born in that open. Blind, they
nuzzled up to her nipples;

fed while she, nodding, curved
her thick forearms about their bodies.

In this way, and snow floating
all among the black mass like stars

in a sighing sky, the infants grew.
When at last they opened their eyes,

their mother loosened her fur
and they climbed to endless morning.

They saw points of green in the snow,
they tasted the wind. In April

the cubs found the end of the forest;
in May, examined the blossoms

on the chokecherry trees
near the falling wall.

When I was cutting the grass,
a huge black bird,

like the devil descending,
shaded the house, the porch.

Running, I saw glistening fur, bears—
or was it the bird's wings,
overlapped? The twin shadows
of the men mending fence?—

Another, another, two more
joined the soaring circle;

then returned to the ancient woods.

The Future

There was a great tree, gigantic old oak,
across the lane's ditch, just before a fence
that outlined the bleak, snapping-turtle creek—
Darkness stirred there, like a snake, through green.

We children invented futures in that marled
palisade, adopted acorn babies—
infants who did not cry, complain, whine;
who required no thrashings.

In this *present*, this *not*, lawns are unmowed,
troughs rife with weeds and despond,
dust blowing up leaves like accusers' voices.

The oak, its pocketed offspring are gone,
seeds flown downward, questions unanswered.

Dog Girl Tells the Truth

Where I breathed, every day but Saturday,
was deep in the riot cave behind the stove.

I lay there, paws splayed toward escaping
heat. Mother said *No* but the family dogs

barked and licked. Of course the games couldn't
continue, though I tried to shift my shape,

adapt my limbs to the floor. Father begged,
then dragged me by my pelt, the chastened pets

keening like wolves losing their young. I cried
for fire, for tongues, for fur, my nailed toes

abrading linoleum while they dressed
me in red chiffon for the prom they'd planned.

A Hunting Story

The Saturday hunter meant well.
He meant to kill the jackrabbit
jumping from rotting corn stalks
in the winter-rimed field.

Confused, the old black spaniel
forgot she was a hunting bitch;
became the hunted, the white tail.
She jumped, too.

The bullet from the .22
Got the spaniel clean in the chest.
Her heart's blood burst to snow,
to stalks, to furrows.

She died in slow black circles.

I sat straight on the wooden chair,
comforting the spaniel's daughter
and crying, crying. Linoleum roses
grew red at our feet.

This happened in another time.

In the evenings, when I tell
my city-provincial dogs, they stare,
then run in happy circles and fall,
glad, on the Turkish rug.

Rhomboid

Always in a hurry, that shape—its parallels boxed
yet propelled, navigating an unresistant deep—

The '59 Chevy, Flamingo Pink, sharply finned
ship, belonged to my boyfriend's father. And
wasn't it unique?—bench seat angled back, just
the right petting pitch, brazen windows cracked to
let in Iowa's 30-below cold (we'd heard sad
stories about other winter lovers who, heater on,
forgot). The midnight road, frozen flat, north to
south, silently aimed at Orion, his burning belt.

Our farmhouse was axis-bent, like Dorothy's, by
a long ago cyclone, the lean-to kitchen precarious.
Upstairs, our bedroom walls inclined to eaves, and
the coal shed, out back, graded itself in slanted
ranks. Was that where I learned momentum (I was
startled, once, to see myself in a city window, head
ahead of torso, diving into the noisy sidewalk);
was this the source of my rush to the end of things?

That boy, sweetly flat topped, Old Spiced, pinned
willing me to the herringbone upholstery while I,
craving his Viceroy kisses, upleaned at him. Our
breath flared like Northern Lights on the audacious
vehicle's windshield. But that boy wasn't enough:
I was in a hurry, on course, requiring distance.

He—no doubt a fine upright citizen in some
Midwestern town—seems to lean against
the car's tropical sheen. He drags on his cigarette,
stubs it out, and, opening the sloped door, waves
goodbye; unlined eyes calm, eternally smiling.

Black Rock Forest

The grasshoppers copulate, so intent
that I could step on them; they could go back
to soil like the politician who,
while laboring happily over
his mistress's blasé flesh, leaps from life,
heart burst like a jungle blossom. Among
the rampant goldenrod the yellow spider
hangs herself, her web a ladder to death's
order, mate long since dispatched. The forest
is in love with repetition: watchers in
flowers ready themselves for morning's
Climb out of your bodies! Then, like eager
grooms they arise from their blossoms, part of
the mountain's fruit, the feverish silence.

The Corn Field

I hard–walked
into the green sea daily,
into the damp center,
on the black bottom soil,
where the corn started up
each night, restless every night.

I stood, crowded,
fighting for air,
confused
by disappearing crows
and the feel of leaves
on my skin, my dissolving skin.

I was drowning
in the corn.
I was up to my chin
and I was drowning
and no human was there,
but the prairie wind,
the big blue wind,
was blowing everywhere,
all the time, through time.

And the wind,
the flat blue wind,
sighed, covered me,
took my air, closed me.
Then I drowned in the green corn;
in the dark green corn,
under the black loam
is where I drowned.

What We Reap

—to the memory of my grandfather, W. F. A. Rabe

Who can tell what silent Wilhelm thought,
squinting at leaves like fingered roofs
against the sun, the limbs that grew them,
the whole hickory woods—a part of the farm
he'd bargained for. Perhaps he savored
the feral taste of rock-hard nuts, the shagbark's
function; heard his dead mother's voice,
old country-heavy, a black forest in it.
Will spared the ten acres. He farmed; passed.

The new owner quickly cut and sold off
the ancients; he traded forest sovereigns
for get-rich corn. Within weeks, with planned
precision, the enterprising grower starved
the nearby, mud-lush slough.
Then he, wielding forecasts of substantial
profits, disciplined the irascible creek.

Say that the hickories, the slough, the creek
are branches of a time tree that can't be
killed; like dowsing sisters they've led us
to this drive-up, end-of-century bank,
its monied stanchions. The branches unclasp
hands, deposit spoiled fruit in vacuum tubes.

Turkey Buzzard

Unable to lie, the vulture points out truth:
he descends to scavenge tread-deaths,
the fox's spoils. Discrete as an undertaker,
he swallows all but the bones.

After dining, he stands a moment,
staring into the open; stiffens his wings
around his torso like a penitent
fixing a hair shirt; then maneuvers
his earth-ugly bulk up, away from his work.

End feathers lifted, span eagle-wide,
the sin eater transmutes, he becomes the sky's
most exalted fixture, an angel
risen out of something's last long pain.

In parts of Medieval England, after a death, the body was laid out
with a plate of food upon its chest. A local outcast, the "sin eater,"
was paid to eat the food, the act symbolically granting absolution.

Buck

August: the final Sabbath, the cherished
mountain. Against a blowzy full moon,
an array of antlers. Incautiously

I approached. The buck bent
one startled leg. I stepped harder,
summer's grasses riffling and breaking

beneath my sandals. The buck swung
his wild grave head and broke: earth
thundered, dead stems shaking. I

followed but he traveled too far.
I turned and maundered below, along
the armored garden, its brocade of beets

and chard, rustling dry vines; into
the tame yellow eyes of the house.
The next night I tried again; laid

myself on the deer's own slope,
in the moon's steady beam; waking,
waking to the flawless circle. At

times, a star punctured the vault.
The buck avoided the terrain.
September's sky: moonless, with wind,

rain-precursing, percussive wind.

For the Girl Buried in the Peat Bog, Schleswig, Germany, First Century, A.D.

She always walks
the dark world, head skewed
to the cry of some sorrowing bird,
left arm outflung,
right enfolding the birch branches
that arranged her death.

They blinded her
with a band woven from the colors
of fire and sun and soil, they led her
to shallow waters and made her lie down.
They laid a plain stone
over her nakedness.

Her eyes closed
from the force of color and her face—
delicate, forever fourteen—
forgot her lover; found,
in the long violence before dying,
the expression of light.

Deliver her,
sight restored, to her northern gods.
Let this child's body grow back
into the earth; eyes rest
on luminescent roots,
her final darkness.

Goldilocks, Grown

In the middle of my life, I came to myself in a dark wood.
    —Dante Alighieri, Canto I,
        The Inferno, The Divine Comedy

Can't seem to get the fire going.
Too much trouble stoking it, piling on wood.
Flu, in belly and bones, keeps me cold.

Three windows, each crowned
by three leaded, beveled panes,
bend cedar and fir, their everlasting reach.
My body hurts. A light rain falling.

When I was a child, on the farm,
Mother briskly handed me a dish—
blackberries in sugar syrup—to ease
a stomach ache. I ate the fruit, one glossy cap
at a time; lay back on my parents' pillows.
I watched the furrowed old walnut,
line trees between flat expanse. Slept.

Out here, as far west as I could risk,
I'm sick. The fire is fitful—everything else
provided—chair, bed, a bowl of soup,
sudden rainbows over stacked books.

The always trees talk, limbs crossing.
A dark wood. The wind in the canopy
                calling, burning.

TWO
Like Night

Whence comes the sound of the jade flute, flying through the dark,
Coming with the spring wind, hovering over Loyang?
On a night like this to hear the song of "Willow-breaking"—
What else can I do but think bitterly of my home?

> —LI PO
> "On Hearing the Sound of Flutes at Loyang
> on a Spring Night"

Truck Stand

Sultry July; month ajar. Aunt Bonnie
speaks and her brother, my father is there
in the air of the market stand. Cars sound
along macadam Raspy voice, hint of
a smile. *Thank you, come back.* Hands heap brown
sacks—sweet corn, sugar peas, string beans. Uncle
Frank, Walt, Ken, Grandma—all wording it, all
at once. The sun, beating down the John Deere.

Such a longing they had—and what they got–
broken hearts, burnt crops, bad deaths. I wanted
Bonnie to talk, talk, talk; keep Dad conjured;
he, absently taking my child hand.
I beg them back—those gone prodigals; their
sweet hapless speech outvoicing resilience.

By the Side of the Road

Bathrobe askew, sash awkwardly knotted,
he reaches the road just as the delivery man
thrusts the daily at the yellow tube.

All night he tossed and turned;
their blankets wrested off, rousing his wife.
He claims she tried to push him out.
Maybe he's right. Other events clutter her sleep:
she finds herself settling, becoming old;
she limps through their rooms, left foot dragging,
as if she were her grandmother. The season irritates:
its damps flute her bones and she hunches,
losing her long neck to the chill.

The neighbor's rooster crows. Stars shrivel.
Yawning, her husband's startled by what the glass
reflects: his loose face, gray hair lank on forehead;
his body, worn out, an affront. All day
it will come to him, this mirror shattered.
His wife, leaning against the kitchen counter,
will long for her grandmother's pancakes,
a new oilcloth, a round table, anywhere else.

Tonight, they'll attempt, again, to be gentle;
bypass truth just enough to cross over,
kindle remembered likeness.

Lessons

At sixteen I cut into the worm, I
contemptuously dissected the frog,
laid out on mirrored metal—I saw my face.
Who, you ask, will kill the cat that murders
the bluebird's chick? In the doomed orchard
dying trees forget how they edged toward
bees, convulsed to fruit. High in the woods,
beneath the hawthorns, the skirted brambles,
deer the color of dying leaves turn and
turn and go to sleep. The clock in the kitchen,
time-swollen, ticks. I talk to the dishes,
the immortal cats. Days like this, the dew
dazzling the sky, it's *all* beauty to me;
even the stopped wing; the bent, wet grass.

Emily, in the August Garden

A warbler child flits through the wire fence,
flaps, then perches on the sunflower's face;
sings. On my face, a vagrant, southerly
wind. Our garden senses its end—squashes
straddle the path, test the gate; tomato
vines tilt from their fruit's weight; beets bulge raised
beds. Potato tops degenerate, green
to umber to black. In the west, late sun
pushes aside thunder heads, drenches me
in gold. Last night's dream featured a colossal
snake, then many, all white, writhing, in a
ditch; showed our house, ornate facade cast off.
I woke to weeping. Now, at this late hour,
I am deep as earth—a meadow, thriving.

Emily, Going Somewhere

You know about sight, sound—the clock ticking
intent, weeds outgrowing peas, the lonely road.
You accept interference. Call yourself bold
but you will find, when at last you reach the
door, that you are your own restraint. Return
to the room's center. Watch the spider shroud
the fly. Listen to the scratchy cries, small
violin screams. Remark the winding sheet.

Leave. You will return—how can you avoid
your future? Mount the wooden chair, witness
up close the spider crocheting—niggling
housewife, so good at her work. Now note the
grasshopper caught in the cat's wide smile.
Touch the carriage's door. Just try it. Go.

Indulgences

Carlo died. . .Would you instruct me now?
—Emily Dickinson to Thomas Higginson,
on the event of her dog's death.

The murk, again—and black bevies,
like birds, like Ur-serpents—
feathered heads whipping, beaming
above the canopies of moving coaches.

Always, now, the gone companion, eyeing,
through gloom, flourishing filaments—
fixed, praising his immense dark.

And these words, jagged, distancing pinions,
semblance of dog, my burly black brother—
barking, barking from grassy gardens,
sweet archaic smile flickering—
                these bannered indulgences,
                    sweets I cannot resist.

                    —*to the memory of Luke, a dog*

Walled Garden

Who could love this book of hours, fruit
trees trussed and bound to sandstone walls?
November constricts the vegetable plot;
blackened mass of beet tops. The lettuce
attempts fealty, but weather will finish it.
What the garden seems to desire is a return
to gracious conditions—peasants in white
smocks cultivating marjoram and parsley.

I run into lumped firewood every
time I unlatch that black gate. The garden
anticipates my departure; its cruel, susurrant
gossip can't wait. Still, I return, again and
again, watching ripped clouds, blundering into
piles of leaves. In the greenhouse, it must be
told, grape vines let go interlaced supports.

What this garden needs is less green, more
hardy plants, a woody stock—who will advise
the steward?—cobblestone paths. Who
will rake, till the soil? Cold silence is what
these walls, the garden now own; and wind,
rooks, jackdaws—. Over there, in the far
corner, where grass bedevils the foundation,
someone tries to mend—see the needle?
thread?—the broken pages of autumn.

March, Ides

So aware of it—the gray-to-white
phenomenon, illegible advance—
it's a cloud, a plow
making, pushing vapor, the purple trees
behind it skiing toward mirrors—

Perhaps this breach represents
time (x) time; that is, 2 (x) the instant,
2 commencements at once
collided and embraced—you,
unlikely force, lodged
in a green foursquare, on a mountain,
at the apogee of the frozen
Delaware, the Susquehanna—
How oddly we achieve what
we finally are—this modest domicile,
for instance, similar to the house
your mother and her twin grew in,
now settled, a little shabby, the one you,
at hope and despair's juncture
(overlooking parallels) chose—

One cat rests its tuxedo chest
on your bedded knee; the other,
fore (four) limbs folded, gratified,
naps on the garden carpet—

As I was saying, she said, *2 cats*
upstairs—akin yet opposite; the one
on the rug black as jet, face flat,
pupils vertical slits, unlike and similar
to the goat's squared-off dashes,
the cat's own tail as it flick flicks—were
you ever frightened (she asked) by
those Toms who murder their sons?—

Double time. Time folds here,
you can hear the crease—and downstairs,
not one but 2 thinking machines,
allotted equipment for 2 humans
at the near millennium, plus 2 black dogs
teaching each other Night's echo,
2 more (newly-counted) cats gathered
near the pale gray philosophers,
modems duplicating and
augmenting, time (x) two-four,
a Gregorian murmur—

The cloud noise backtracks
as the plow, returning, emerges from
the vanished horizon—scraping
the other, equivalent roadside,
its dead grasses.

You say, *Nothing (y) makes sense?*

And, now, a little something wet—
       Must it? The snow,
              the sleet, again?—

Looking

In the dawn
I saw stars reversing clouds, I saw
clouds pretending to be sky, and
a jet's plume speaking. This was
winter, in a place where seasons teach.

Later, when
the mountain tilted, the sun shone,
but it was still eight below. The cold helped
the snow to stay pure, helped the hills
outline themselves beyond my window.

The road
contributed to the whole idea
of perspective, yet I understood how
the ancient painters leveled everything,
how vision was only an autistic's dream.

While I looked,
the dogs rhythmically chewed their bones,
until the daily news was delivered
by the small car with the yellow sun.
Then they barked.

Winter Flies

Through winter they lived,
temperature-stupid,
sluggish as autumn bees.

They floundered
in anyone's hair,
floated in coffee cups.

Their bodies piled up like
leaves beneath
a hundred-year tree.

Now, born out of heat,
the flies gaily beat
fairy wings; they cluster

as if their lives
had purpose; the fleshy fruits
of summer, already theirs.

The Fourth Beast

After this I saw in the night visions,
and behold a fourth beast, dreadful and terrible,
and strong exceedingly . . .

   — The Book of Daniel, 7:7

She stood at the window, elbows bent, plotting nothing.
The world had changed: light edged to inference.
Still, serene, listening, she later claimed,
for the tree frogs' song, the odd howl of a coydog,
she saw two great eyes streaming out of the gloom.
When questioned, she faltered: she saw *something*.
A red tail. A pulsing vein. The thing seemed
to reel down her hill. *Who encroached that smoking land,*
rode her soil so easily? She ached.
The creature halted; lurched forward.
And the woman said to the landing *Now I must go out of light*
but her feet would not lift, could not shuffle.
In the morning she effortlessly
handed the blackness back to the window, which took it;
then, tormented by sudden sun, bulging heat, quartered shadows,
she cowered. Evening returned, its sultry touch.

An interval. *(Had time slipped?)* A voice: plain, friendly.
At that, she insisted, her own voice woke, asked
How could two feet gripped by floorboards rouse the beast,
glare gunned at glass? A laugh from beyond the screen.

High night again. The animal crouched in his grim tower.
He had leapt up, she was sure,
from earth's cluttered crust, sight pointed at her breast.
She tensed and listened; heard no more.
The blaze had gone. *Wait*, she called. *I'm coming.*

Dogs

This morning, a dream of dogs—behind and beyond
the house, like clouds among the spruces—packs of them,
big and beautiful, brooding. Our own companions,
Luke and Lily, pranced, but Gomez's black cat face burred
like an angry capuchin's, his eyes ignited—.

I opened the door. Picked up pebbles, discreetly lobbing
them at the strange dogs, whispering, *Shoo, shoo*, but
they would not leave: they reeled together, a storm gathering.

One, the brindle shepherd, padded over the bluestone
path and raised her long-furred form up, standing, as
Tasha used to, paws heavy on my shoulders. She stared,
perplexed; and sniffed, as if trying to remember my face,
my reek. I was afraid, but at last she glossed her muzzle
against my cheek; she tasted my forehead, leaving the prickle
of her tongue; then dropped down and rejoined the others.
Luke and Lily quietly followed.

                    While I wept,
I wondered: dogs in cults . . . and I said to my companion,
We should notify the authorities, but I knew it was *our* task
to capture the dogs. The blackened cat hissed around my legs.

How? I thought—their elegant large bodies soughing past
the vertical posts of trees; raining through the sutures
we held in our needled fingers.

Jay and Father in Winter

There! A stellar jay in a blue sky,
above a hard river,
and clinging to the creature's back, a woman.
What's left but descent?

—So the jay flies free and
the woman (*she sees!*) lights on white ice,
where her dead father waits.

We know how this ends—
the specter withdraws; the woman knocks
on every frozen tree in the forest;
the jay squawks maledictions
from his perpetual sky.

Her father leaves, again—
that bird evicting him—and worse,
the woman
can't recover those auspicious wings.

The Cat in the Diner

swerves under my table.

I am not surprised.
The prescription for my new glasses
is wrong: surfaces become
colors that move silently past
my feet, walls warp at a glance.

The villagers are calm. They talk
among themselves while
mountains tilt at their town.

I eat my lunch,
reach to pet the stray vision.

Japanese Beetle Trap

The plastic bug catcher
sways on a wooden pole,
its sex–odor beguiling
flighted incandescence.

Pheromone-confused,
the beetles fall in,
can't fly up, can't get out:
tea in a poisoned cup.
The trap, guaranteed
one whole season.

Days pass, the cargo
adrift in heat. I look:
living gems struggling
on their lovers' carapaces.

The curtain at my window
moves. A dry year;
the grass is metallic.
Under the soil–quilt,
in the grainy sea, curled grubs
uncramp eager legs,
swim to scented romance.

Out of the Dream

Bodies on the bed; love cries,
ancient and ecstatic: if I weren't
wrapped in you, ringed by all your eyes,
I would laugh at our mingled
foolishness; this happiness
exploded out of absolute night.
If I were Piranesi I would draw splendors
of sun and shadow from our rapture.

But clouds descend and birds quiet and
I add the morning together:
fog so thick I can't see beyond glass;
a dripping faucet; the hallway,
pointing to another, smaller
hall; a door, then stairs down,
landing that angles abruptly.
I live in a house of corners—
brief, obscured perspectives.

The dog sleeps at the foot of the bed.
The cat pries open the sewing room door;
mist skeins the passage. A car
breathes by. I pull the quilt;
alone, I'm cold.

Yesterday we two
flexed the broken day to us,
we changed the whole air to suit
our dappled mood. Love, I accept
these waking inversions.

Night Song

*As to Nightingales—they are almost as numerous with us
and as incessant in songs as frogs with you.*
    —Coleridge in a letter to a friend

The peepers sing; they shrill their love,
and stars perforate the world–dome.

We pull apart: moonlit, your chest and chin,
your eyes. You glint in and against the glow.

All the troubled stumble through the doors
of their days; they speak old illusions.

We lie sleepless, then sleep, our night sight
breathing life to dead events.

In the garden, seeds separate clotted soil;
they reach and reach for sun.

Yesterday the crane flapped over the waves.
I looked up, was blinded by brilliance.

You tell me the deer, dying alongside the road;
I show you a warbler, talons curled neatly

on turned soil, brittle fingers, feathers
torn: a collage, a stilled life.

There is a barrier between us: a thick,
cryptic glass; our fingertips cannot touch.

The peepers tweak the blue–black cloth of night.

THREE
Landscape with Wings

The man preaching on the Crescent
asked me, "Where is God?" I knew,
and told him. He shook his head. He disappeared
in the great whirlwind that snatched houses and men
and hurled them up, up, to the pitch-black sky.

—EUGENIO MONTALE
from "Wind on the Crescent"

Truman and Me

At noon on Wednesday
I saw Harry S. Truman
walking across Fifth Avenue.
I knew Harry,
alive again, wearing
a double-breasted,
off-the-rack,
gray serge suit,
properly buttoned.

Harry stopped,
resisting the force
of pedestrians, and
looked at me, looking
pleased through
steel-rimmed glasses.
I could read
the President's mind—
a cyclist who waits!
I smiled back at him,
felt my grin
grow to both ears,
splitting my face in two.
Harry laughed,
then saluted me.

I could almost
travel to Hiroshima
on those rows
of good-natured teeth.

Rapunzel, Rapunzel

She wants to discuss morels,
needs to describe
their musky scent,
pungent taste—how good
mere mushrooms can be when cut
from the damp
beneath prairie trees.

My friend explains—
pale hands eloquent
in the restaurant air—
how she soaked
the ghostly cones in brine,
rinsed, then drained
them before closing
their cratered eyes with flour;
she sautéed them in butter.

She carried some back;
they're drying on a line
strung from wall to window
in her city kitchen;
saved for winter.

Like the good wife yearning
for the forbidden rampion,
I crave this delicacy so much
that I would plead
my husband into theft, promise
anything to the witch.

Nor would I give
a moment's thought to the loss
of our unborn child
when that fine magic overtakes
my tongue again.

The Tortoise

A recluse who
now and then sought company,
she would appear in the center
of the living room rug—
hoary stone politely
inquiring after lettuce.

Allowing herself
to be held, tendriling
her wizened neck from its shell,
she frowned and
preened her beak at
the touch of fingers.

Once, on a garden outing,
she mistook herself
for a turtle and climbed
the wading pool wall.
We found her,
water-besotted, among
the baby's floating toys.

That autumn she
crept into the closet
for her seasonal death.

She slept right through
spring, beyond resurrection.

Elemental

—for my mother

By logic it's fire I hate: heat that destroys;
unstoppable, vermillion teeth. But I don't remember
the morning our house burned down, its few furnishings
vertical licks—the table, velour chair,
their wedding Fostoria melted to its beginnings.
And we small sisters, clinging, crying
in the fringe grass while our mother pumped water, heaved
buckets—the feverish rubble, scorched galaxy.

She tells the story—how she managed to save
the console radio, the Singer sewing machine; how our father,
home from the night shift, found basking ash, bent tin.

I should despise fire but I'm drawn to flame,
the way it enhances, then reduces all to essence—
his arms holding us, holding her; all four of us harmonious:
fearful and relieved. The cornfield flourished
round the smoking plot, the war in Europe raged;
even the crows wheeled and cawed outside our little circle.

Survivor

He shot movement, November branches, but
the dusk he got was my brother; his son.
When he saw what he had done, my father
used his gun, again, to join the dead.

My mother and I stare at opposite
walls, across forests of dumb furniture.
Our home's halls are treacherous: my brother's
heart, father's mouth detonate as we pass.

Mother is constant in her mourning. Through
the kitchen window she sees black trees; sets
the wooden table, each night, for four;
launders Father's hunting jacket, each week.

I tend our fields. I have no father,
brother; all I survey belongs to me.

Widow

Envious of him who plunged
into early rest, the farmer's wife gets up

from radio nights, wanders stale rooms;
she pleads his name out of the gloom.

The widow's own, benign ailments come and go
like visitors bringing similar gifts,

repeating phrases in pained tones.
When she calls at the nursing home

(despising the hard chairs her friends
are fastened to, the mortuary cleanliness),

she worries that the door only opens *in*.
The widow sees burials in the eyes

of her grown children and she offers
family artifacts, mutely beseeching,

> *Take these, for I go*
> *to the farthest meadow;*
> *my feet grow roots.*

But the farm is leaving *her*.
The garden, untended, wilds away;

the barn razes itself, chamber
by chamber, its raw rectangles

allowing the seasons entry.
It's been years since the farmer's wife

crossed the threshold, handed grain
to living creatures. Her children

lower their looks. The striding,
strong figure they recollect

passes by months now—
back hunched, eyes as faded

as her husband's overalls,
still hanging in the back closet.

Crowd

When you push shut the silverware drawer, you can hear them:
inhabitants of your home far longer, the dead complain about your
housekeeping; they set the porch rocker going until the telephone

repairman notices. All vortex, they increase when disturbed,
attracting relations, old friends who, edgy at first, grow bolder
and bolder: only unseal attic trunks and Flora's downstairs,

sweeping, picking up the beads the children broke and scattered,
collecting them in her apron. Push hard the barn's sliding doors—
there's Frank on the high beam, a mote in the strawed light.

The old man leaps off, masses into blizzard, howls up the neighbor's
lane. He climbs his chimney to save again the burning house,
his dead sons agape. The ghost's seared feet crop up, shards,

in each spring's garden. Every night Emma and her cousins pick
up gravel or lizards in the road; they plan gardens with stolen rakes.
Like a tour guide, Will points out the land's first foundation;

its boundaries heave, baring the center—slabbed rocks, like trees
banked for planting. The dead will never be finished, you will join
them. In the northeast bedroom you will frown at sleeping guests,

your blurred fingers rearranging blankets. Your fingers will part
the metal blinds; travelers will detect a cramped light, displaced
shadow. From time to time you'll give off a little turbulence.

To the Starling
in the Winter Raspberry Patch

If you are dead—and you must be, husk flesh-
empty, long time laid here in snow, caged by
dry canes, scalloped feathers still flashing gray
clouds—if you don't perch, anymore, on the oak's
sad branches, ruled by an exalted math,
you devotee of balance; if you have
lost your charged heart to the marauding cat's
perfect arc or winter's cynical cold;
why, then, when I position your ruffled
crust alongside my ear, do I hear song, gilt
notes; feel a ragged tremor, as if your
wings tautened, took off? Why, Starling,
do I search for just one of the seven
invisible threads connecting me to you?

Angels

1. *One Way*

Truly, friend, angels aspect in a tallow sky,
on a surging, turbulent ribbon. Their chariots,

lit like lions' eyes, ride amber beams.
Unfolding like stairs, the angels glide

on ruddered feet, yellow hair gusting.
You think, Go. But the hour detains you,

angels in their gowns rustling louder
than the brief, papery din the living make,

countenances more terrible than executioners'.
Awkward, trembling, you open

the door of your concerns as undulant
shoulders feather evening. The beings near,

usurping the motion you intended, majestic hands
explaining, *No clemency*. Then the archangel,

man-maned, azure-garbed, swallows
the shimmering wind, vanishes. Your vision

is heightened. Quaking, punished to the marrow,
you hide, like Rembrandt's poor old Tobias,

granted sight. One motion commences another.
Wheels turn, circles curve, and the angels

of the yellow hair gaze icily from the interstices
of arced eyes. You are lost.

II. *Otherwise*

The angels materialize sooner, you recognize
their coming. The sweets you stole

as a child are miraculously returned before
the clerk registers their loss; you do not

(*not once*) founder; lie with the wrong man;
or weep. Divinity punctures your heart

with the ease of a hummingbird opening
the flower's face, wings whirring in summer's

supernal gold—flare that ministers and
singes. Your bones resonate like harps

in wind. Cherubim greet you, proclaim you
Innocence. Isn't this all you yearned for?—

and your own shoulders, friend, sprouting
the most enormous wings!

Landscape with Wings

This beats all, she thought, yesterday we sang like
angels for the new priest, our rural church's schism

for a moment mended by—*Godness*? Lord, I want
to love this winter luminary—mirrored fence mesh

waning sky substantive windows—your hand,
liturgical pattern in this your model home, where

all men, husbands or their doubles, carefully escort
wives down every January ramp. The pastor smiled,

a benison. Someone's clothesline grips someone's
flower-basket quilt, its abundant, layered cloth

confirming the wind's chill route; the frozen, sloping
garden below it. No simple, footed woman, her

fingers stiff, pinned that stitched warmth to icy
wire, to be viewed against this divinely austere sky.

Two Poems

. . .*Inside you*
there's an artist you don't know about.
He's not interested in how things look different
in moonlight.

—RUMI

I. Dry Spell, August

The parts that can be watered are green; the
rest—seedling trees, shrubs—shriveled, charred.
All that you planted threatens
to leave for dust.

Long time now, long time saying farewell
to body, to limbs burning out of dreams. You
are the nun you envied; desolate as the bone
the dog found in the crackling orchard.

II. January First

Evening's sickle eye turns on earth's curves,
the roofs of battered and broken barns. Trees
shuffle, then fix the horizon;
branches tighten.

You are distressed. The artist mentions
the splendor that outlines your body. Deaf, blind,
you lie down inside the clutter of night;
your consequences join you.

Together you sail a visionship between
blades of sleek grasses, brambles that puncture
the moist quiet. Tall white birds
narrate your way.

You roll in your sleepboat, and all your
neglected parts miraculously accommodate your
torso. Now you have become your issue;
they are you.

The artist adores this transformation.
The artist knows what's what. Forget the wings
you wish, the season you think you need.
Get up.

County Meath, Ireland

I had to get up early
before he came
out from the house;
I had to move quietly
so I wouldn't wake the watchdog.

I had crawled under the gate,
patient as a fox,
after the farmer
left his fields at dusk.
Circling,
I asked the hedgerow's permission,
lay down close to the undergrowth,
my body pricked by the stubble
of summer's last crop.

At dawn I awoke, soaked with dew
and dreams of passage graves,
of runes hammered into stones
standing and declining
all around great green mounds.
The lapwings wavered
in the lightening sky.

I was looking
at everything twice that September.

Place

—for Ernest

At eight, anemic, undersized, I sat on textbooks to read
the blackboard, rolled-down maps. Afraid
to raise my hand, ask to be excused from the room,
I wet myself, the stacked words, straight wooden bench.
The harridan must have taught spatial affinities
while I changed into clothes brought from home.

How far was California from Iowa? Where was Home?
How big India compared to England? Although I read
and read, I couldn't grasp bearings or affinities.
If I could find the right heading, I would no longer be afraid,
I knew, but True North could have been a bench
to me, constellations forfeiting the tedious classroom

air for polished oak. Grown, I left my dawn-facing room,
the prairie I believed in for the citied wilderness; quit home
to follow my own ley lines. High-rise apartments, other bench
marks along the streets weren't directional signs to be read
but sublime and puzzling patterns. I tried, but I was afraid
I would never master the complex city's affinities

to graphs and guides. At last I gave up that place for affinities
that promised clarity. And I found you. Now, in every room
I visit, I pinpoint east by remembering your face—not afraid,
no matter the globe's curved coordinates. You are my home.
The postmark on your letter tells me your location. I read
it, looked at the photos while sitting on this morning bench

in a faraway country. The strange, high bed faces the bench
and the southeast window, as our own does; affinities
I've mastered. I extract your demeanor from your letter, re-read
the words. It's cold here; an alien fire warms this alien room.
You sleep in our bed, on the second floor of our mountain home
while I, here, write poems. Sometimes I find you beside me, afraid,

chest heaving, brow knitted. I confess to you; I am afraid.
I gently shake you till you wake. You get up, sit on the bench
in your coat, and we talk until it's time you went home.
The moon moves through Scotland's wild autumn sky, affinities
changing among planets and stars as I, in my small room,
wait for the gray day dawning, trying, again, to read

the sky, its portents impossible to read. Not afraid
anymore, I consider, in this room, on this foreign bench
how our affinities are aligned, how soon I'll be home.

In the Catskills

Even the hemlock grows
indifferent to life; dies
standing,
keeping his secret
for untold prideful years.
The tree's needles diminish,
bark and heartwood
degenerate
to dust.

When the north wind
hears of this, he offers
a parting kiss,
and the tree falls
into the arms of his fellows,
who carry the corpse
on their gnarled shoulders—
a hundred years procession,
a stately bearing
back to the mountain's body.

This Much

All honor to the mist: light
quivering behind wafer cloud;
light, suffused; milky white
to saffron. A heron nods inside
the blur; wings above and below,
languid blue flags in the edgeless
hour. An evening primrose,
prodigious in its white-veined
leaves, impatient for dusk, fans
the ivory haze. The heron's call
rasps the floating dawn.

Blue Sky

In my dream
there is a breathing blue sky
stretched taut
behind white rooftops
with gray walls falling.

I want that blue.

Before me
mounts a clay bluff
finished by grass beating
green against the sky.

I need that blue.

In my dream
I run right up the clay
and the pounding blue
smacks me flat
between the blades.

I love that blue.

A white bird
carrying his own light
hangs reasonably
in the sky, watches me
with one red eye.

I think
I will call this home.

Wildlife

I. Meeting

I always had it in my mind to visit the bears in their natural habitat.
I wanted to give them my sandwiches and celery sticks.
On one occasion—it must have been in October, for everything

uplifting has always taken place in October, perhaps because
of the blue leaves gyrating bleached skies, the funereal cries of gypsies—
three deer, wearing bibs and top hats and little else, sauntered over.

Naturally, I photographed them—they were charming; their blonde
antlers twigging the formidable, brushed beaver; their laughing amber
eyes. Two bears squinted out of the woods; asked, blushing,

if they could be included. Of course, I replied. My plan was to place
them all on the cover of my latest book. I asked around—
Is this appropriate? Will it look good? The bears and deer agreed
to every pose, provided they could have seconds on provisions.

II. Losing

I find I am being detained. More important, I can't remember
where the wildlife live. Two men in one body point to a yellow house
on a cliff. I seem to see furred faces in the streaked glass of the dormer

windows. The men are, of course, corrupt—two heads, four legs and
arms—but we all crowd out the door and climb into the waiting limousine,
my darling daughters in the back with me. Many people are seated

up front, most fondling maps, all giving directions. Then I see them,
in the rear view mirror, the bears—they're waving from an ashy knoll,
the dressed deer rearing up beside them, knocking top hats against

the beeches. They appear to be crying. Though I protest, we drive on.

Changed Places

Sitting at table, surrounded by faces, waking voices.
Eight in the holy morning.
This chair upon which you've never before rested—
this four-legged, turned maple apparatus—
set, here, in the guest's place.

Light, sudden and slow—light, counting the rooms,
today's inhabitants—through the window,
where still stands the 100-year maple,
ridged skin turning green,
burls bulged like saints' quaking eyes.

Green, this end-of-May moment—
and these faces, filled; voices, wavy with light—
you, strange visitor,
have never before seen; never will, again.

Eadfrith on Lindisfarne

O at last I am completely happy, heart turned back,
—arms ricocheting off the corners of the great
partitioned earth!—The other novices above the grass

smile down at us, mouths twitching the litany. When
our feet stop—Cuthbert and I—meteors shower our
cassocked bodies; iron rays shave the pages of the books

we have made. All our words lift in thanksgiving.
I am promised to my teacher's god, learning
by the hour how to be speechless inside revelation.

●

And now, over the boiling ocean, dragons among clouds!
The saint and I climb out of our cleft pit, calmly piss
in sheep-cropped grass. Thorny wings crackling,

the creatures descend like comets; their fiery tongues
scourge our fringed hair. The child in my body cries
for my irreclaimable mother. But Saint Cuthbert

hushes my mouth; that old man guides me to quiet
rooms, where I lay down my god's words, for the rest
of my earthly life, on the skins of consecrated calves.

Eadfrith was the scribe of the Anglo-Saxon Lindisfarne Gospels,
produced for the enshrinement of St. Cuthbert's body in 698 or in
response to it. Eadfrith became bishop of Lindisfarne in 698.

Author Biography

Bertha Rogers's poems appear in journals and anthologies and in the collections *Even the Hemlock: Poems, Illuminations, and Reliquaries* (poetry and visual art, Six Swans Artists Editions, NY, 2005); *The Fourth Beast* (chapbook, Snark Publishing, IL, 2004); *A House of Corners* (Three Conditions Press, Baltimore, MD, 2000); and *Sleeper, You Wake* (Mellen Press, NY, 1991). Her translation of Beowulf, the  Anglo-Saxon epic poem, was published in 2000 (Birch Brook Press, NY); and her translation of the Anglo-Saxon riddle-poems from the *Exeter Book, Uncommon Creatures, Singing Things*, will be published in 2010. In 2006, Rogers received an A. E. Ventures Foundation Grant for excellence in writing and visual arts and for contributions to the field. In 2003 she received a Ludwig Vogelstein grant. In 1992, she founded Bright Hill Press, Inc. with her husband, Ernest M. Fishman. Her website is bertharogers.com.